The

Silent

Voice

Life Lessons through Poetry

ChaseMore, LLC.

Atlanta, GA

1

The Silent Voice: Life Lessons through Poetry

Credits:

Editing: Cynthia L. Ryals, CPC, CSC @ Evolved Life Soutions, LLC.

Photographer/Creative Consultant: Michael A. Frazier

Graphic Designer: Danielle McGee @ Good Lookn Co.

Published by Chasemore, LLC.
5800 Oakdale Rd. #145
Mableton, GA 30126

ISBN-13: 978-0615984742 (ChaseMore, LLC)

ISBN-10: 0615984746

This book is dedicated to my children, Morgyn and Chase. You will never realize how much joy you have brought into my life. I only hope this book will give you an understanding of who I am and the person I want to be. And know I will never stop trying to make a better life for you in every way.

Love forever and always,

Daddy

<u>Special Thanks</u>

It would be unfair not to acknowledge certain individuals who helped me when I was in hell. When I resided in the darkness, you were there for me. These are the individuals I consider as more than friends but family. I know I am not the easiest person in the world, but they never judged me and had nothing but encouraging words for me. So Chris, Terrence, Sunny and Mike, from the depths of my heart I thank each of you for accepting me and never giving up on me.

To my brother, Terence, thank you for the words of encouragement. We had our rocky moments in life, but you have ALWAYS been there for me in your own way. For a person like me, you are a great big brother and outstanding uncle.

Lastly, to my Princess, you made my words a reality. Because of you I found out who I am and what I can be. I don't live by regrets. I live by life lessons and I thank you for all the lessons I had to learn from you.....0430.

The Silent Voice: Life Lessons through Poetry

Introduction
Chapter 1 – Playing Games
Chapter 2 – Meantime Man
Chapter 3 – Where are You?
Chapter 4 – Just Give Me a Minute
Chapter 5 – Torn
Chapter 6 – Look at You
Chapter 7 – Appreciation
Chapter 8 – Can You Explain Love?
Chapter 9 – Untitled 1
Chapter 10 – The Past is the Past
Chapter 11 – Give Me a Chance
Chapter 12 – Unwanted Dreams
Chapter 13 – Come Over
Chapter 14 – My Offering
Chapter 15 – My Sunset
Chapter 16 – Walk to Me
Chapter 17 – Side by Side
Chapter 18 – Seasons Change
Chapter 19 – A Sad Thanksgiving
Chapter 20 – Come and Gone
Chapter 21 – Untitled 2
Chapter 22 – Made for Two
Chapter 23 – Unseen
Chapter 24 – Unclear
Chapter 25 – Two Heart Beats
Chapter 26 – Life
Chapter 27 – I Am an Asshole
Conclusion

Introduction

At an early age, I was surrounded by older men who were very loud and opinionated. But the best thing for me was they let me hangout with them. Even though I shouldn't have seen, heard, or partaken in some of their activities, I learned a lot. By simply keeping my mouth closed, listening to the stories and observing my surroundings, I was able to form my own opinions about life.

At the time, those men didn't understand what kind of impression they were having on me, but they laid the foundation for who I would become -- good, bad or indifferent. I took those life lessons I learned from them, as well as my own life experience, and began to write. For so long I had kept quiet about what I thought, but then I finally found an outlet that didn't require me to speak. Hence the title, "The Silent Voice." I am a quiet observer of life with something to say.

It was not initially my intention to write a book. Years ago I started modeling, which led to meeting people in the music industry. The more I learned how the music business worked, the more intrigued I became -- especially with song writing, or rather, the *money* song writers made. At that time, my mission in life was the pursuit of money; nothing and no one else mattered. So I decided

I wanted to become a song writer, which meant I had to actually *write* something.

I took the first leap and began writing. My first work was personal; things on my heart and mind that I never shared with anyone. Finally I had a stage to express myself without actually having to say it myself. Becoming a song writer became my passion. I believed it was what I was meant to do. However, when the product was complete I wasn't sure what to think. Would anyone like it? My biggest fear was to share myself and it not be received well. I wasn't sure if I was ready for that type of rejection.

Needless to say, I never became a song writer, but I didn't stop writing. I had found something I was very good at and it came effortlessly to me. I wrote of personal conflicts, dreams and ambitions, and my thoughts and perspectives on love and life. I was even able to share my writings with others. But it was years before I would attempt to do anything constructive with my poems. I believe one of the lessons I learned was that I wouldn't do much in life if money was my main motivation. Now my motivation is simply to share. No longer will I keep these words to myself or hidden in my desk.

The purpose of this book is to use my thoughts -- transformed into poetry -- as life lessons to help others. It has been 12 years in the making. I believe I had to endure turmoil as a way to prevent others from having to follow my path of mistakes and mishaps. My sincere hope is that you will be able to relate to some of the events or circumstances within these pages and discover something that helps you in your life. If this book impacts one person's life, I will have made a huge accomplishment. I believe that if we are not impacting others or leaving our mark, we are not truly living.

I have to share a story I've told several people over the years. It's amazing how the smallest things we do make the biggest statements in our lives.

I had just moved back to Atlanta after living in Detroit for a year. I was in the process of looking for a job, but having no luck. After about two weeks I was getting very frustrated and starting to second guess myself; thinking I made a mistake by leaving Detroit to pursue a modeling career. One day, after I received another rejection, I was walking back to my car with my head down trying to figure out my next move. For one brief moment I raised my head and made eye contact with a lady sitting at a stop light. In that moment when our eyes connected, she simply took her hand and pushed her head up. I couldn't do anything but shed a grin. Not one word was shared between us, but that simple motion of her hand -- reminding me to lift my head -- has stayed with me for years and helped me many times.

Never again would I get so discouraged that I hold my head down. Of all the encouraging words I've received from people, none have stayed with me and helped me in life the way this woman's reassuring gesture.

I don't know you personally and we may never meet, but my hope and prayer is this book reaches you in some way, and that you can one day share with others how reading this book has inspired you. And to that lady, whoever you are, I thank you for the little things. It is the little things that have helped me become who I am and who I will be.

Chapter 1

Playing Games

Playing Games

You want me just as much as I want you
The difference is I show mine
All you give is that quick glance
While I sit and stare to express myself
It's funny
How cool you play the game
Cause you wondering if I'm feeling you
So I get another glance
Just as fast as the first
But this time
I'm gonna make my move
How do I start this conversation?
I can't just walk up and say my name
I wish she would just come and make herself
known
I do know
I'm tired of the same game
Would you stop looking at me?
Just come over

How many signals do I have to give out?
Damn
You are fine with that sexy ass look
Hope this ain't another one
Trying to get by off his clout
I can already see how this is about to happen
He'll look all night
Thinking about what to say
And just when I get to the door
He suddenly wants to talk
Expecting me to give more
This is it
Another game of cat and mouse
I wish I could get up the nerve to say hello
It's just the game has worn me out

Look at these two poor little souls
Both are thinking the same thing
But neither knows what to do
If they only knew what I knew
They would understand the rules of the game

It has nothing to do with what to say
Or what you're supposed to do
The reality is
It's about you being you
Unfortunately pride has won another round
It has taken two souls that were meant to be
Two souls that should be one
And sent them their separate ways
With nothing left
But curiosity

Chapter 1 - Playing Games

Everyone has played the eye dance. Two people go back and forth just looking at each other and wondering what the next move is. "Is he going to come over and say something or just keep staring?" "I wonder if she is just looking for somebody to buy her a drink". These types of questions go through each other's mind for possibly an hour or so. All the while, 'Cupid' or 'Love' is sitting there laughing at these poor souls. With the fear and doubt in their hearts, they are potentially passing up on their true love or soul mate.

Fear is a common emotion of humans. The biggest challenger to fear is confidence in oneself. There is no rule to say a man has to make the first move. I understand that women want to feel wanted or pursued, but sometimes a man needs a little assistance--a simple smile or friendly gesture to let him know it's alright for him to come over and speak.

Day after day, people continue to play games and it gets them nowhere. The hardest part of meeting someone is the initial introduction. Once that is out of the way, it's easy sailing. Just be yourself and let the chips fall where they may. This may or may not be your soul mate. The only way to find out is to stop playing games.

Chapter 2

Meantime Man

Meantime Man

Never meant to feel this way
Never meant to fall so deep
Just thought I could make you happy
The one to make your life complete
You just used me for your meantime man
While they fooled around on you
And made you feel insecure
But once they came back
It was my heart kicked to the curb

In high school they never saw what I saw
That's why I wanted you for myself
A friendship was all I could get
Always wondering about our first kiss
We grew up to see life different
But I looked at you the same
I saw the woman you had become
Wondering why you couldn't see me
As the same man

Longing to touch your cheek
Or hold you in my arms
A friendship was all I could get
There was a deeper feeling I couldn't resist

Calls came everyday
With your voice on the phone
Another story about how wrong you've been
done
All the time
Thinking in the back of my mind
That it's me you long
Crying on one end
Feeling the tears on the other
Is this how it happens?
One friend calls another for comfort
One friend falls so deep
He wants to be her lover
Realizing that at the end of the call
You're not the one she'll be thinking about at all

We moved on
Went our separate ways
Trying to make the best out of our situations
You chose another that brought you hurt and
pain
And maybe that pain will heal one day
Remember that one day there was someone
Someone who thought the world of you
Who gave you a pedestal to sit up high
I guess I'll just forever be known
As your meantime man

Chapter 2 – Meantime Man

We never get exactly what we want in life. When it comes to the person we want, we have stipulations or requirements that are like piecing together a puzzle. He has to be this height, with this kind of job, no kids and never married. She has to have a nice body, real hair, be a freak in bed, and not trying to get married. Whatever it is we seek, we have a hard time finding that one person. That's when we find ourselves trying to put together one perfect person through multiple people. These people fulfill needs or desires we have in our requirements.

Here's a classic example: Consider the needs of a woman. She can have one man whom she dates. She allows him to take her out, spend money, and have good conversation; but she is not feeling him like that. Another man is her associate who comes over after the date, or she meets him for a nightcap. Sexually he fulfills her needs. He has a nice package and knows how to use it. The last man in her life is the one she calls after the date and sexual escapade. His title is, "the friend." Now to be honest, this may not occur in a given evening, but the end state is the same. It's difficult to find the friend you want to date and who can put it down in the bedroom. You may have to compromise and invent one. But be careful because your requirements could be skewed. What you have been looking for, or even the one that is the fit for you, might be right in front of you. Your meantime man may be your everything man.

Chapter 3

Where are you?

Where are you?

We have never met
I heard a lot about you
You have giving to so many
I've been passed up though
Almost we have come close
Not quite eye to eye
Don't know what I need to do
Only wish I could let out a cry
Why punish me so?
I heard what you have is good
Every day is bright
Every night is just as clear
You are just hard to find

Many say they have met you
Others really don't know
For me I just want to know
Why?
Let me feel this power you possess

Let me see the other side

Have I been blind?

Have I let you go?

If so, please come back

Because I really didn't know

Show me what I've missed

What so many hold true

Give me another chance

I can't go a lifetime without ever meeting you

To be honest

I've seen your bad side

How much pain you bring

That's my biggest fear

So much hurt I've seen

It's really not fair

This magic power you have

So few get to enjoy

So many get hurt by the wrath

We'll talk one day

And you'll have to explain to me

But right now
What I want to know is
Where are you love?

Chapter 3 - Where are you?

The expression, "I don't need a man" or "I don't need a woman," is completely false. When God made Adam, He also made Eve, Adam's partner. There is no way we can go through life without someone from the opposite sex. We simply were not built that way. We are genetically designed for each other.

Society puts us in an independent state of mind where we think we can do this alone, but there is no way that we can. There is nothing wrong with looking for a mate --that one person who will complete you, push you, and grow with you. Do we come across people we feel can do these things? Yes. Should we give up because we failed a few times? No. The purpose of those failed relationships is to understand what you will and will not accept, and what you may need to change about yourself. This is where self-reflection comes in. But the key is to believe he or she is out there.

In many regards, our issue is that we are looking for someone. When your primary goal or motive is to meet someone, you will find it hard to maintain a healthy relationship. In particular, some women feel they have a biological clock and must fulfill certain criteria to feel complete; this is understandable. We all have life goals we want to accomplish, but we still need to take our time to ensure we are in the right place, right state of mind to be successful. You can find your life partner in your twenty's or fifty's. When love is ready to be found, love will show itself. In the meantime, you have to prepare yourself for love and what it has to offer. If you do not learn from those past relationships and do some self-reflecting, you will be asking, "Where are you?"

Chapter 4

Just Give Me a Minute

Just Give Me a Minute

Every time I see you
I know you are mine
It gives me a feeling I never known
A feeling where I don't what to be alone
All I want to do is make you happy
Give you all the things you deserve
Wipe away your tears
Hold you close on the rainy nights
When the sun is shining
Taking walks in the park
Talk about everything on your broken heart

Just give me a minute
It's all I need to figure it out
Just give me a minute
To see what our love is really about
Just give me a minute
That's all I need to figure it out
Just give me a minute

I don't want to have no doubt

I never meant to take you for granted
Or leave you alone on all those nights
Just had to make sure you were the one
The one I could be with the rest of my life
You understood my ups
My downs
Support me for every little thing I do
But I need more time to think about
A minute to think about me and you

Why can't you understand?
This decision I made for us
I want you to understand
You are the one who stole my heart
I need you to understand
My head is filled with so much doubt
But you have to understand
You are the one I can't live without
Simply because I Love You!

Chapter 4 - Just Give Me a Minute

There is nothing wrong with admitting that you are not ready. It is better to be honest than unfair to someone. You also have to be thankful when someone is really expressing who they are. Does this mean they are immature or naïve? No! It means they are honest with themselves, but don't want to lose you. They realize who they really are, but also know they have some work to do. This is their opportunity to give you a choice of whether or not you want to wait until they get things in order. But you have to be clear on what it is they are not ready for. For instance, some men like to be financially stable before they engage in a long-term relationship, while some women may feel they are not over a past relationship. It's up to you to determine what you will and will not put up with. Some people want to assure they will be able to give you their all, instead of just leading you on.

As any new relationship begins, we have to use a certain amount of patience. The way we are patient getting to know someone, we must have that same patience as the other person prepares themselves for a long-term relationship. But you have to understand what it means to be ready for a relationship. Have them provide you with their plan. This way you are not wasting your time and/or energy on someone who is not committed to you.

Everyone has room for improvement. We just have to make sure we are on the same page. If you see potential in this person, and you are ready for a long-term commitment, just give them a minute to prepare themselves for you and your future.

Chapter 5

Torn

Torn

These last few weeks have been hell

Shit has been weighing on my heart and mind

Over and over again

Trying to figure out which way to go

This way or that

Up or down

Left or right

Backwards or forwards

Two hearts reside in my decision

See I am torn in two

Two ways

Two women

Each with a different agenda

Or maybe it's not their agenda

But mine

I can't continue playing with emotions

Theirs or mine

Something has to give

These sparring matches have to stop

Because the bumps and bruises are becoming

too much to bear

In the red corner

The single mom

A friend I've had for a few years

Time spent

Conversations had

Shared sweat in the late evenings

And the kid

I love the kid

But this is my friend

She's tried countless times to move us forward

Only to be seen in my eyes as my friend

Can't say I haven't thought about it

But if I can't be faithful

I can't be committed

More I pull her strings

Toying her along as my sexual puppet

I'm the puppet master

Cause in my mind

She already knew the score

Deep down she knows I can't be what she needs

Because I told her

I'm not the one to give her what she needs

What she desires

But does she listen?

Only hoping I'll change

I won't

I can't

Not now

Not for her

In the black corner

The forbidden fruit

The fruit offered to Adam by Eve

Only to neglect God's command

See years ago this one was the apple of my eye

But the feeling wasn't mutual

Time passed

Lives changed

But for some reason the laws of attraction

reversed

You can't fight fate

And we connect

For months we go from after thoughts

To only thoughts

With every day we grew closer and closer

With each conversation we share more and

more

A connection with no connection

Because her connection was meant for others

Unfortunately we can't stop

We can't stop talking

Laughing

Sharing

We can't help this attraction that can't go

anywhere

This has become my best friend

I have found my spark

My fire

A light I can't explain

But yet, it belongs to another
The further our friendship blossoms
My emotions are confused
Each time she leaves my side for her shelter
I am alone
Not just alone as in by myself
Alone as my heart is incomplete
The worst part about it
Nothing can change
She has to go
She has duties
Responsibilities
Roles to play and fulfill
None of which are to me

So I am torn
Torn between both rings
In one corner a woman who wants me
Willing and waiting to be my everything
But can I give her the same?
Am I being fair to her and string her along?

Just in case she may be the one

And in this corner

A connection I've never had

I can't even explain

With a woman who fulfills my every desire

Except her availability

But does she see me the same?

Does she view us the same?

Or do I want to see what I want to see?

Me versus them

She versus her

My decision

My emotion

Torn by the rings

Chapter 5 – Torn

Sometimes we can't control who we fall in love with. Many people believe that if you have spent a certain amount of time with a person, you should love them. Love is not something that simply develops over time; neither is it instantaneous. Society has put a timestamp on our lives. We believe that by this age we should be here or there, and have this or that. For example, because we have been seeing each other for three years there should be a proposal.

The truth is you know you are in love when you know. Man or woman, you cannot deny your love for someone. It will show in a variety of ways -- the way you look at someone; how they remember your favorite snacks are Oreo cookies when it's that time of the month. The little things can speak volumes.

Consider asking yourself some questions before you take the next step:

- Can I see myself with the person forever?
- Can I be fully committed and faithful to this person?
- Will he protect, provide and lead our family?
- Do they meet the standards I have in a partner?
- Is this my best friend?

These are just a few questions to ask before moving forward in order to avoid putting yourself in a bad situation.

There is no time limit on love. Three days to three years to thirty years; once you have found yourself in a position to give your all to this one person you will never be torn; not by time, emotions or feelings. When you make the best decision for you and yours, there is no limit to your possibilities.

Chapter 6

Look at You

Look at You

I've seen you before
Will see you again
But from time to time
I don't want it to end

Staring at your eyes
Just standing in your presence
Breathing your air
Smelling your fragrance

Thinking to myself
What did I possible do?
For God to bless me so
Each and every day
I get to look at you

Chapter 6 - Look at You

There is an old saying: Beauty is in the eye of the beholder. This is absolutely true when it comes to love. Sometimes we can't explain to others what it is we see in someone to make us love them so; neither should we have to explain. They simply cannot see through our eyes. Whether that person is over-weight, unemployed, or has children; it's something about them that *YOU* love. It's the kind of love that makes you want to be in their presence all the time. Through the good and bad, when that special person comes around, everything else stops and It becomes all about them. When they walk through the door your heart skips a beat. When you see their name come across your caller ID, you can't help but smile. As you are walking down the street or stepping into an elevator, you catch a fragrance that reminds you of them and it brings joy to your soul.

Here's the kicker: This person doesn't truly know the special feeling they bring you. It's not that one loves the other more; they just cannot see through your eyes, as you cannot see through theirs. But what you and your partner's eyes do show to each other is that you only have eyes for them as they look at you.

Chapter 7

Appreciation

Appreciation

Have you ever stopped to watch a tree?

I didn't

Ever enjoy a wonderful sunset?

I didn't

Ever sit and think about nothing and enjoy it?

I can't say that I have either

Ever wonder where is she?

Will I find her?

Is she really other there for me to find?

These are the questions I used to ask

I don't have to ask anymore

Because of you

My heart has been found

Now I can enjoy watching a tree sway in the wind.

I can enjoy a beautiful sunset

I can't sit and think about nothing though

Because my mind is on you

You have brought enjoyment to my life

My senses and emotions have blossomed

I have learned to appreciate the little things

Look at a leaf

It was once green

But it goes through a transformation

Just like I have

The true beauty is starting to show

It takes a leaf a while for the real side to show

But eventually it does

Unfortunately, the leaf will die

But the good thing is we enjoyed its beauty

But unlike the leaf

My beauty will not die

Thanks to you.

Chapter 7 – Appreciation

It's the little things that make life worth living. The smallest things -- a leaf falling in autumn; the array of colors displayed on a tree in the blowing wind -- give you the opportunity to see life and death. The life of the leaf has reached its climax but will soon die. This is evolution.

Day in and day out we go through our routines without every appreciating what is right in front of us. Just having another day is much to be thankful for, no matter your circumstances. You don't have to have a big house, with a luxury car and truck loads of money.

When we are in relationships, we must never take our partner for granted. Once someone begins to feel under-valued or not appreciated, they begin to check out of the relationship. The same things you did early in the relationship to catch your partner are the same things you need to do every day. Remind her of her beauty. Compliment him on the project he did around the house. Most importantly, pay attention to details. It's the little things that matter most. People are always looking for new ways to feel alive. It's your job to notice. It could be a new hair style, a new suit, or a hobby they just picked up. You have to take notice and be supportive. At the end of the day, we all want to feel appreciated.

Chapter 8

Can You Explain Love?

Can you explain Love???

How can you show someone you really love
them?
How do you know they really love you?
Is all this really meant to be understood?
I thought I knew what love was until I meet her
This love I have I can't even explain
I can't tell you why or when
I just know
This is a feeling unspeakable
I try to put it to words
But I can't
Can you really explain love?
All I know is when she enters the room
My heart begins to smile
When I look into her eyes
I see my soul
When I touch her
I want her to feel the love through my finger
tips

Can you really feel love?

I feel love ever minute

My heart and soul

Have never seen happiness like this

Thanks to her

I have happiness everyday

I only wish I can explain this feeling I have for

her

Can you explain love???

I hope not

Because I love

Chapter 8 - Can you Explain Love?

Most emotions have a cause and effect. You accidentally touched a hot iron and the result is pain. A family member passes away; bringing hurt, which allows you to cry. One day you come home from work and find your house burglarized, causing anger. Each of these emotional examples has a cause and effect, but is there one for love? Can we honestly name one cause which produces the effect of love?

We often use the expression, "I love you," but what caused us to say it? Maybe we don't want to hurt the other person's feelings, so we reply with the statement. Perhaps when

60

you were at your lowest moment, they were there for you when all others turned their backs. Or could it be when they're in your presence you can't help but want to make them happy? You can't think about anything but them when they are away. When your peers notice a change in you, they feel moved to ask what has brought such happiness.

With love, so many causes combine to result in the feeling of love. As love goes, there is never one cause as with other emotions. Sometimes we want to spend so much time trying to identify, understand and explain love, but why? An emotion so strong, so passionate, so life altering, and with so many causes; would you really want to explain love?

Chapter 9

Untitled 1

Untitled 1

I could never forget the day
You came into my life
I knew from that moment on
Every day would be so bright

As I stared into your eyes
Wondering what to do
Knowing how I really felt inside
All I wanted to say was a simple 'I love you'

As our days turn to nights
And the sun starts to set
I still feel
And will always feel
Like the first day we meet

Chapter 9 – Untitled 1

Certain moments in life are unforgettable; like a first kiss, or landing that first job right out of college. More importantly, we never forget the first time we laid eyes on our true love. We remember what they were wearing; the fragrance that radiated from them when we were in their presence. There was something about them that was hard to explain. We just knew right then and there they were the one--our soul mate. Our very existence became all about them. Each and every day meant something special because we could share it with them. And in sharing we need to always express our feelings with a simple, "I love you."

Chapter 10

The Past is the Past

The Past is the Past

What do I have to do?
To prove that I'm true
When I say to you
That you're the only one for me
I don't go anywhere
I don't stop and stare
Lately I feel like
You're blaming me for what
I use to do

I'm not a perfect man
I'm doing the best I can
But please don't judge now
Just let the past stay in the past
These girls don't mean a thing
I don't care what they think
I make this vow to you
Just let the past stay in the past

Last night

We had another fight

And again

You couldn't see my side

I wasn't at the club

Back in the VIP

I don't care what your girl said

This time it wasn't me

Is it so hard?

To forget the past

You and I know

We can make it last

I can't keep going on

With your insecurities

The fact of the matter is

This relationship is about you and me

Chapter 10 - The Past is the Past

Can we truly forgive and forget? We often use the term, "baggage," to explain people's issues. These are the issues people carry around from relationship to relationship. Moreover, they take out their frustrations for something someone from their past did to them and blame the new person.

Before we can feel ready to move into a new chapter of life with someone, we need to honestly reevaluate our circumstance and decide what we learned from our past relationship and if we are ready to move on. It's not fair to your new partner to take out your past experiences on them. They have no idea what you're upset about. All they think is they have done something to upset you. You need to stop acting out before you lose something special.

Another common issue is moving beyond the past. Once you and your significant other have resolved an issue, let it go. There is no sense in harping on the past. If you agreed to move on, forgive him or her for whatever occurred. You have to remember the past is the past. As the saying goes, "Today is a gift; that's why it's called the present." We need to focus more on what we have in front of us and how to become a better person. Our future is only determined by how well we deal with the past. So let the past stay in the past.

Chapter 11

Give Me a Chance

Give Me a Chance

See me for who I am
And not who I used to be
Understand this change that I've made
And you will understand the person I'm going to
be
Look deep in my eyes
And see what's in my soul
Just give me a chance to show you how much
I've grown
I'm not yet who I want to be
But each day is a new day
For me to mend what has been torn

Day and night
I think of how things should have been
And all I see
Is an emptiness that needs to be filled
With joy and happiness
Not hurt and pain

You took away that emptiness with just your
touch
Now let me show you your true worth

I was traveling a road alone
No guide to take me forward
Or bring me back
All I have is myself and my God
Then you came into my life
To make up for others slack
You've dealt with my up and downs
My faults and my virtues
The closer we become
I see me for who I really am
I look to the fallen sun
And my road has brought closure

Chapter 11 - Give Me a Chance

Is it safe to say we are all trying to become better people? In our own way, we are attempting to become more than who we were or who we are now. No one is perfect, but we demand more of ourselves in achieving our personal goals and aspirations.

In relationships, we need patience and understanding. We do not come to the relationship having reached the pinnacle of our perfection. We require from our partner a chance to grow into more than who we are now. The simple fact that someone understands their shortcomings speaks volume to who they want to become. And who are we to not give them a chance just because we have work to do as well? After all, actions speak louder than words. So as you see this person trying to improve themselves; not only for their benefit, but that of the relationship; step back and give them a chance.

Chapter 12

Unwanted Dreams

Unwanted Dreams

I'm sorry you had to find out this way
But if not now, when?
When you realized that I can do wrong?
And will this be the day your life comes to an
end?
I wanted to tell you for so long
The words just wouldn't come out
I really wanted to make you happy
It seems I really ended up hurting myself

Why did you have to walk through that door?
Why couldn't you just have worked late?
Why do I have to be the man I am?
And for once, admit I made a mistake
She didn't mean anything to me
She was just something to pass the time
Unfortunately time has run out
Cause I couldn't resist

You saw what I wanted to say

So I know the pain is twice as hard

But the funny thing is

Who really hurt who?

You see me

In this bed

Destroying what we built

I see you

Walking away

Leaving me deep in my guilt

How can I say I'm sorry?

How can I ask for forgiveness?

Please forgive me

Because how can I say goodbye?

I lost all that I hold precious

Never mind the house

The cars

The money

I lost my life

In a single stroke

In that one agonizing push

I looked up and realized my life was over

The next day as I awake to my useless life
I turn to see my dream has been deferred
Here you are
Sleep in my arms with a smile on your face
Letting me know I really didn't make that fatal
mistake
Was this some way of saying my dream can
come true?
Or was it my way of saying I can never go on
without you?
No matter what the dream meant
Or the others to follow
I know
Here and now
I can never be unfaithful

Chapter 12 - Unwanted Dreams

Even while we are asleep, our minds are still in motion. Unfortunately, as much as we may try to control our thoughts, even during sleep, it's impossible. Trying to think about what you would do if you won that $300 million dollar jackpot, or living out some type of sexual fantasy never goes the way we plan. Why? It's because subconsciously our thoughts and motivations come to fruition in our sleep. One case in point is experiencing the loss of a loved one -- not in the sense of death, but the ultimate betrayal of infidelity.

One of the ultimate sacrifices is to give yourself to another, forever. To be with only one person sexually is hard for most to comprehend. But when you take those vows, those are the commitments you are making to the other person and God. As humans, we have needs and desires we want to fulfill, but we still have a glaring eye -- especially men. The statement that men are visual creatures is true. However, the defining issue is acting upon their physical longings. So those who wisely choose not to act upon their lustful desires must ensure or submit to the fantasy through their dreams.

As if they are acting out a movie in their mind, they set up the scene; from beginning to end, they tell the story of what they want, desire, and crave. But even in their subconscious, they understand what this act of betrayal means. They comprehend how one bad decision affects the other person. A dream that seems like hours in the making, in reality, only lasts a few seconds to minutes. And as easily as the dream began, the relationship could end. We all have our unwanted dreams.

Chapter 13

Come Over

Come Over

Come over to my place
For a night of ecstasy
Come over to my place
Tonight's about you and me
Leave the kids at home
So we can be alone

My place in your resort
To fulfill your fantasy
Just think of my place
As a world where you are free

Come over to my place
I have a bath waiting for you
No need to worry
My tub can fit two
Come over to my place
The music is playing real low
Come over to my place

Now let's move to the fireplace

Let me see your eyes

Tonight I have a big surprise

Come over to my place

I'll meet you in the bedroom

Just give me a few minutes

To do what I got to do

I got your favorite flowers

Candles all around

Watching you stand there

I know it's our time

Come lay next to me

It's time for a new life

We need to make this our place

Cause I want to make you my wife

Chapter 13 - Come Over

One simple word -- romance! Where has romance gone? Today, we live in a microwave society where everything has to be instant. Our food, our communication, even our relationships must happen immediately.

Sometimes we need to step back and relax. Let things happen according to its timetable, while holding on to high expectations. And these expectations should come from the woman. Men should follow women's directions. But if women do not require romance, they will not receive it. If women are accepting whatever it is men are offering, they are mostly at fault (we'll get to the mostly part in a few seconds). It's alright if you want to be sexual beings, but still have a standard on how you want to be treated. If you act un-ladylike, don't expect him to treat you any differently.

Now men, you need to learn more about women than how to get them in the bed; learn how get into their hearts. Even if she doesn't know any better, show her how a lady should be treated. Open up her car door, even if you are the one driving. Ask her what she wants to eat when you're at a restaurant and then place her order. When the two of you are walking down the street, walk on the outside close to the street because this is the gentlemanly thing to do. And when you do get her over to your place and you know the evening will end in the bedroom, set the mood. Let her know you appreciate this moment. Visually express it is all about her. No matter what she has going on outside, when she comes over, it's all about her.

Chapter 14

My Offering

My Offering

I can't say I offer perfection
But I offer my heart
I offer to grow old with you,
Build with you,
And love you and only you
I offer to understand without judgment
For it is the Lord's divine word
My offering is to be a better man
Cherish and enjoy each day
As though it may be my last
Every day is a gift from God
And I must celebrate in those gifts
But lo and behold
One of his greatest gifts was you
So I offer compassion and a loving ear
Because for the next 50 plus years you will see
Each day is a new day
And all my offerings here on earth
I offer to my one and only queen.

Chapter 14 - My Offering

In our lifetime, we have opportunity to leave our mark here on Earth. We each have something inside of us to give. But do we know what that one thing is? Have we tapped into our true selves to understand what we are meant to do? Whatever that special aptitude is, there is something we can offer in our relationships as well.

When two people come to the table and decide to be in a relationship, each has something different to make the bond function efficiently. Opposites attract and, once each person identifies those opposite qualities, they can begin to understand how to make them work in their favor. For example:

- He likes to keep things neat and tidy. She is more of a clutter bug.
- She is driven and always trying to do more, whereas he is content with his position in life.
- He is *always* on time. She is *always* late.

These are just a few differences people can have; however, it does not mean one person is better than the other. In extremes such as these, the best offering is open-mindedness. Even though two people are on opposite ends of the spectrum, when they come together, they should balance each other out. You have to open yourself up to adjusting to the other and be willing to come out of your comfort zone.

Each relationship is different and comes with its challenges. Even though we have perspectives, it does not mean we have issues; only opportunities. It's an opportunity to grow together as one, and recognize each day that you have something special to offer.

Chapter 15

My Sunset

My Sunset

It's breathtaking

It's calm

It reminds me of your eyes

A peace that is hard to describe

The day has passed

And it's time to enjoy

Enjoy the life I've been waiting for

The coming together of different worlds

It's not quite orange

It's not quite pink

With a hint of yellow

But together they meet

And slowly they join

To make a beauty most can't appreciate

I can

And I will

Understand

That each day

Everyday

I will end the day
With my sunset

Chapter 15 - My Sunset

One of the most beautiful experiences we can have is to view a sunset. At the right time of day, in the right place, it can bring a surreal calm over you. The uniqueness of the sunset is the variety of colors coming together to blend perfectly, harmonizing into one.

When two lives come together, they have opportunity to become a beautiful masterpiece. But unlike colors of the sunset, a relationship requires work. Two people may be on opposite ends of a spectrum. It's like the old saying, "opposites attract." The key word is, "opposite." Whether it's different life experiences, different challenges, or different backgrounds; they can all be a recipe for disaster if work is not put into the relationship. The most important thing to understand is that we are all different, and there is nothing wrong with that. The question is, are we going to let those differences destroy us?

The upside is that you have someone to teach you how to look at things differently. Here is the opportunity to learn new things and get a fresh perspective, instead of how you have always done things. Your strengths may be the others' weakness. Admit it and learn from it. This is what can help make you a successful team. Admittedly, this is not something that happens overnight; but with enough will and determination from both parties, you will be able to enjoy many sunsets with each other. No matter what goes on in your life, when the day is over, you still have your sunset.

Chapter 16

Walk to Me

Walk to Me

I stand in front of you today
Looking in your eyes
And the thing I just realized
Is that I can see my future
I can see
Each and every day of my life with joy
Pain and hard times are sure to come
But this thing we have here today
Will always overcome

Our day is so clear
The sun shines on your angelic face
To watch you walk to me
Let's me know
My hurt and heartache will vanish in this place
I don't know what can come of our life
I know every day will be a special day
Because you are mine
And we are one

No one thought I would be standing here

Waiting for my life to change

I put my heart on the line

And it seems you were the only one who cared

So walk to me

Slowly

I want to watch you

Come to me as only you can

Show me that my time alone was worth the

wait

Here you come

Closer and closer to me

I feel the lump in my throat

And a tear begins to form in my eye

Fear and joy

This is what I wanted

So finally it is said

And I pause to reflect

Three things I know on this day

With my mind I say 'I trust you'
With my heart I say 'I love you'
With my mouth I say 'I do'

Chapter 16 - Walk To Me

Out of the three hundred and sixty-five days of the year, there is one day you want perfection. It's that day where nothing can go wrong and it's all about you. The weather is perfect. You have on the perfect dress. All the people you love are there with you, and you are about to marry the perfect mate. Yes, it's your wedding day. But do we really understand why this is the perfect day? Sure you spent months planning. You spent a lot of money on flowers, the photographer, the venue, etc. It's the special day because your life is about to change forever.

A year or so ago, you decided to marry this person and all that comes along with him or her. You made a promise to love this person for the rest of your days. But that was just a verbal commitment. On your wedding day is when you make the ultimate promise to God -- to love, honor, cherish and obey this person. This is your last chance to hear those words from the minister and decide if you can love this person through sickness and health. Can you support this person for richer and poorer? Until death do us part? This is your final chance to say yes to all these questions in the eyes of God. As she is walking to him and he waits for her, you're both caught up in the moment. But the reality check is your vows. There is no getting around those. So with conviction, as the walk is taking place, understand your perfect day is just that; a day.

After your perfect day is over, this is when the

walk of life together begins.

Chapter 17

Side by Side

Side by Side

Slowly I see
My angel appear to me
Glowing like the moon above
For everyone to see
Caramel colored skin
Hazel brown eyes
With a body built
To make a grown man cry
Take over my soul
And all I possess
Nothing means more
Then your gentle caress

No one ever knows
This feeling I keep inside
Your presence alone
Makes my joy come alive
Knowing our hearts beat as one
And you standing by my side

Makes me want to give in to you
And show you my real side

Nothing means more to me
Then this moment that we share
Holding you close in my arms
There's no feeling to possibly compare

Chapter 17 - Side by Side

If and when we decide to get married, we must recognize marriage is a partnership. Everything in the vows, except obey, is 50/50. From a biblical perspective, the man is truly the head of the household; however, he should consult with his wife before making any decisions. The final decision will reside with the man, but she can give advice on the situation and probably reveal some things he didn't think about; hence the term, "partnership." The two of you are in it to win it together, as a team. Every great team that has accomplished great things and won championships never had one person doing everything. Each person on the team had responsibility and a role to play to reach their final goal.

In the beginning of a relationship, people like to put on their "representative"; a mask. But sooner or later you have to be who you are, flaws and all. With your mate you can be yourself without judgment -- from how you look when you wake up in the morning, to how you eat your food -- this person loves you unconditionally. And whatever your physical preference, they have your undivided attention. They make you want to be a better person. But at the end of the day; whether the bills are piling up, or you have all the money you need in the bank; nothing can ever compare to walking this life side by side with

your soul mate.

Chapter 18

Seasons Change

Seasons Change

I'm tired of trying to figure you out
So tired of giving my love
Every day the same old thing
Home alone
Cause you're always gone
Too many lonely nights
Too many broken hearts
I make this promise to you
My season has changed
And not with you

People come
People go
Lonely nights I had the moon
Every season has to change
Well my season has come
And not with you

Crying days have passed me by

Can't believe I left your side

Winter days never felt so warm

Why o why did I stay so long?

It took a while to figure it out

What the season of love's about

When the rain begins to pour

Time to move on

Can't take it no more

People come

People go

Lonely nights I had the moon

Every season has to change

Well my season has come

And not with you

They say April showers bring the flowers

Sunny days we hit the pool

In fall the leaves are changing

One thing I know

I can make it without you

I'm stronger now and it's so clear
Life is not to live in fear
But to be together to grow as one
If you don't think you can make it
I can make it alone

Chapter 18 – Seasons Change

People come into our lives for a reason. Whether the relationship is intimate, a mutual friendship, or a strong bond we have formed with someone; they serve a purpose for a certain amount of time. Many of us use the term, "season." Just as seasons come and go, so do relationships. When it comes to some people, their season in our lives may last longer than the typical relationship. Just as seasons bring something new and different, so do our relationships.

During the relationship we never think about how long this will last. We then take the relationship for granted, not realizing this person serves a purpose in our life. Initially, we will not understand what the purpose is, but it begins to become clearer after the relationship is over. Instead of feeling hurt, pain, and loss, we need to step back and reflect on the experience. Whether the relationship lasts two months or two years, there is something to gain.

One life lesson is not to have any regrets. All of our decisions have both a consequence and a lesson. What did I learn from this? What do I want to take from this? If you can answer these questions, you have learned something which can help you later in life. As we continue this journey we have to enjoy each day as if it were our last. Each relationship is a change of season, bringing newness to our lives.

Chapter 19

A Sad Thanksgiving

A Sad Thanksgiving

I can't say farewell
Saying goodbye is just too hard to do
Because it is bittersweet
But what I can say is
With the distance we had between us
There's one thing I always knew
I could always feel your concern
Your comfort you shared from afar
I could always count on you
To tell me how and what it is you saw

You were an angel here on Earth
Now you are an angel above
Joining so many of our fallen
Who have given so much of their love
Now I have lost another love
A love that was spread by miles in between
Even though I'm sad to lose this love
I'm thankful to have one more angel above

Chapter 19 - A Sad Thanksgiving

Two things in life are certain: Death and taxes. Of course these are two different extremes, but they are realities. One we expect every time we get our pay checks, buy food, or purchase any item -- there is always tax associated. Death, however, is a completely different animal.

We try to prepare ourselves mentally for losing a loved one, but it is impossible to shed the pain. Reflecting on this person's life and what they meant to us makes the pain even harder to bear. We must bear the pain, and there is nothing wrong with that. However, we have to understand that this person's journey has come to an end with a better beginning; although we want to be selfish and keep them to ourselves. But when it is time for them to ascend to the Lord, be sure God has a higher calling for them. They are becoming soldiers in God's army, watching over us.

This is how God is everywhere. The loss we experience actually becomes another soul watching over us. There is joy in knowing that one other force is guiding us in the right direction. So with accepting death and loss of our loved one, we can call this our sad thanksgiving -- the assurance they are looking after us.

Chapter 20

Come and Gone

Come and Gone

The first day we met I had your back
You could do no wrong in my eyes
You brought me up to be a better man
You showed me the things I needed to evolve
That confidence in myself was something I
couldn't see
It took me a while to realize the better me
Two souls that were connected is something
hard to find
A relationship that was built 'til death do us
part
So why did you betray the trust I gave?
Why did you make me look like a fool?
The things I did for you showed me who was
who

Could we get any closer?
This is something I couldn't see
Once by myself

All alone

The next thing I know it was you and me

Though we had our problems

Division tried to take us apart

But this relationship was meant to be

Is it possible to say that this is destiny?

Unfortunately you found another to replace me

To fill a void I couldn't

To give you a comfort you felt you deserved

Just remember one thing

It was you who called

It was you who wanted to be true

Where should I start?

Should I say that from the first day I loved you?

Or should I remind you of the pain I had to

endure?

To know you will always be in my life

But the hardest person to understand

It should have never been that way

You were supposed to be my guiding angel

Instead you guided me to the deepest darkness
of my soul
Searching for a love that should have been
there
But a compassion that was not going to be seen
To hear your voice of inspiration is something I
once dreamed
Knowing no matter what goes on in my life
I will always have you
It's a shame my dream will never come true
A world of me and you
Side by side
Laughing and hugging
The only thing I hope is you know
Know how much I love you

Chapter 20 – Come and Gone

A bond is something shared between people or groups that form a connection between them; such as an idea, interest, experience, or feeling. In life we develop strong bonds with people for various reasons. Many times those bonds are so strong, so deep, that nothing and no one could break them, except the people within the bond. For whatever purpose, bonds can come to an end. If we share similar interests, beliefs or even blood, how do we break our bond? Only those involved can answer this question, but we can learn from the experience.

Any time you develop a connection with another and lose it, there will be feelings of hurt and loss, but it can be channeled into something positive by attempting to understand the good this person brought to your life. Somehow, some way, they left us with a life lesson. Even though they have come and gone, we move on, thanking them for those lessons.

Chapter 21

Untitled 2

Untitled 2

Every time I'm feeling lonely
Feeling like there's nowhere to go
I think of my baby
And realize that I'm not alone
When I look at your picture
And see your face
Then think of the good times
We shared in this place
Over and over
Again and again
This can't end
A relationship that was heaven sent

We know tomorrow may never come
For anyone
As long as were together
Forever
We are destined to grow
There's no one to blame

For anything we've ever done

We've made our mistakes

Just want you to know

I love you so

Chapter 21 - Untitled 2

The harder we love, the harder we fight.
No relations are without disagreements.
Whether husband and wife, girlfriend and
boyfriend, or best friends; there will always be
conflict, because each person is an individual.
They think differently, see things differently,
and form their own opinions. So of course we
are going to disagree because we are not
seeing eye-to-eye.

Sometimes when we push and push, we
tend to push the other person away -- not
because we want them gone; we just want to
get our point across. However, somewhere
during all the cursing, arguing, and name

calling, someone says, "Enough is enough. I don't have to take this." We can call it pride or whatever we like; the point is, things get out of hand, and it's not until the other person is gone that we realize what happened. Was all this worth it? Why did we start arguing to beginning with? You can't even recall how you got to this place.

Now, every move you make only reminds you of them. It could be their face in an old picture, or a smell you come across that makes you think of them. You could be watching TV and see their favorite show and begin to reminisce. The thing we call love brings hurt and pain. The important thing to do is, once you have it -- truly obtained it --

realize what you have, and understand what

you need to do to make it work.

Chapter 22

Made for Two

Made For Two

I always think about those days
With your love on my mind
Hoping that one of these days
You would show me what's inside
To have you take me in your arms
And make me feel secure
To know all the hurt I feel inside
Would leave with a "I Love You'

Every night before I go to sleep
I pray for a better world
A world free from hurt and pain
A world I hold inside
To give you everything I ever owned
It's only half of what I owe
Hoping you feel the same would bring me joy
For once we are unified

I want to drown the seas of Abraham

But this world has made me cold
A strong man I am
With a woman but does she know
That the oceans run so deep
For all the pain you've endured
Tears could never replace
This love I have for you.

What you have inside is made for two
Something not meant for one
What you have inside is made for two
Could you share it with someone?

Chapter 22 - Made For Two

It is a big responsibility when we decide to bring a child into this world. They didn't ask to be born, so as parents we have to provide them with everything they need. So often we give them what *we* think they need, but we don't realize what *each child* actually needs. Some children need coddling often, while others may not need as much attention. Some kids need to hear their parents say they love them, instead of just showing it through clothing and shelter. Just as the person you decided to have children with has different needs, so do the children.

We all sometimes go through changes in our lives, but we must realize what we are doing when we bring a child into this world. I don't think we give them enough love to fulfill the future. We're so worried about pleasing ourselves, but we need to start pleasing them a little bit more. So let's give a little love -- a love made for two.

Chapter 23

Unseen

Unseen

There is no perfection in the world

We only settle for what we can

I looked in her eyes and saw hope

I saw the possibility to open my treasure

This thing I have to hold

For the moments of dawn 'til dusk

You were mine

My comfort

My future

But perfection does not exist in this world

Through the struggles of change and virtue

Time wouldn't permit it to be seen

The person you once were

Satan with his deadly kiss

Seas didn't part

No oceans began to roar

With the fire in her eyes

And the pounding between the hips

We all fall short of the true goal
And that is a love that will never unfold
Pull back forever that thing I cannot hold
For most who believe in love
This will be another story that goes untold

Chapter 23 – Unseen

As we begin our journey of pursing a relationship with someone, we are going in blind -- we don't know what we are getting in to. We do not know anything about this person, so we are flying on blind trust that this person isn't crazy or going to take us for granted.

A lot of people, especially women, go into situations with their guard up. Can you blame them? Time after time they have been through the same situation. They fell for the representative. The representative is the person the other wants you to see, and once they have you wrapped around their finger, they become their true selves. He is the person who really doesn't open up the door. She is the one who stops getting her nails done and that Brazilian wax you like so much. Whatever it may be, they eventually fall back to who they really are. This is the same person who loved that you spent so much time with your kids -- until it interfered with their quality time with you.

We all fall prey to all the little things people show us in the beginning, but what is real and what's not? You do not have to go into a situation completely guarded, but there are always signs to who they really are. Listen to how they talk about past relationships and circumstances. Get a feel of who they really are from family and friends. People who know them are not sure what representative has been presented, so they are more likely to let something slip. And if they keep you from family and friends, this is a red flag. When something feels too good to be true, it probably is. Just because we walk into a situation blind doesn't mean things are unseen. Before you open your heart, open your eyes and ears for the truth.

Chapter 24

Unclear

Unclear

Sitting in the darkness of night
Trying to figure out what's wrong and what's
right
Trying to understand why this happened to me
Was it his will?
This couldn't have been meant for me
For every night I was alone
Thinking you were still near
All these faces are so dark
They are still unclear

A dark and cold world
Without you by my side
Wondering will this pain last
Or should I look for some other delight
Even though brighter days are still ahead
Things are undone
And still unsaid
But before I join you on that day

Please forgive me for much that I say

My heart was torn too many times
Questioning my life
Or did I need to live
For others to suffer the pain I feel
With one more strike
I must finally give

Chapter 24 – Unclear

The prospect of losing life is unthinkable. It is something no one wants to endure, but we all have to. As we sit alone and reflect on our loneliness, we begin to question life, God and our very existence. These are the moments we need someone to help us through the tough times; whether a family member, a loved one or a dear friend.

We sometimes get to a point where life feels meaningless. Fortunately, this is not true. Life is everything. Would the one you lost want you to drown in your loneliness? Of course not. There is nothing wrong with grieving your loss, but life goes on. We have to pull ourselves together and move on. You may question the reason for your loss, but the ability to enjoy life is still in your control. What you do with it is up to you.

Chapter 25

Two Heart Beats

Two Heart Beats

My heart had one beat
Only for me
With no concern
No direction
No affection
And yet it went unharmed

A chill so deep
A pulse that froze mountains
Many could not understand
But one brought me comfort

With that one there were really two
And my heart had an extra beat
So as time moved us further
My heart beat was now for three

One heartbeat for three souls
Joined together for an eternity

But nothing last forever
Because my heartbeat had an increase

One-Four-Three....
This was once my favorite code
This was my way of saying 'I love you'
How quickly three words mean no more?

There was once a beat
With one beat for four people
There was once a heart
At heart torn in two

Two beats within my soul
For only you and your brother
Two beats of my heart
With those two beats
Never for another

Chapter 25 - Two Heart Beats

This particular selection is rather sensitive and personal to speak on. What will be acknowledged is there is a bond one makes with their soul mate and all that comes along with them. Once a commitment is sealed, a commitment is fulfilled.

Blending families is never an easy thing; especially when one has been dissolved. Many will say it's for the better, or that it's better to do it early while the kids are young. But is there any such thing as early versus late when it comes to destroying a family? Many of us believe we are doing what is best for the children. Sometimes we are, but sometimes we are really doing what's best for us and not thinking about the overall effect this decision

will have on everyone involved. However,

when we decide to become one, make sure

there is a true understanding of what *ONE*

means.

Chapter 26

Life

Life

I sit in front of my judge and juror

Alone

Broke down to the worst rages I own

With only one thought

How'd I get here?

Not so long ago I stood in front of the Almighty

to confess my faith

'Til death do us part

But still I sit here

Alone

With no support

No defense to speak in my behalf

Because all I worked to preserve and protect is

being taken from me

With a couple key strokes

A few signs on the dotted line

How'd I get here?

What have I done in my life to deserve the

turmoil?

Let me think

Could it be the way I abused women?

Mentally?

Emotionally?

Was this payback?

Using them as objects of my erection

Could it be the way I treated my mom from time to time?

Making her believe it was all me making things happened

And not the sacrifice she endured for me to maintain

Over and over I reflected through my life

As I gazed out the window to the morning grey sky

Not uttering a word in my defense

Because there were no words to be said

She said them all

Shackled from head to toe

I'm waiting to be told what my sentence to society will have to be

Told when to eat

When to sleep

What to wear

Where to work

How much to pay

They sit there signing and signing

As I look into the grey sky

A mist of rain begins to fall

How fitting?

The longer they take the tighter the shackles become

The harder it is for me to breathe

I wonder if my father is watching over me

If so, how'd he let this happen?

Did I disappoint him somehow?

The judge asks, "You don't have anything to say?"

For a moment my eyes leave the sky to objectify this question presented to me

The piercing of my eyes can say it all

As I look over to my jurors, my judge and the executioner

If I wanted I couldn't utter a word

Because the pain and strife is too much to bear

So slowly I return back to my only solace

The grey sky and mist of rain

Thinking to myself

How is it I made a commitment to God?

For the rest of my life

But this human figure,

This man of law can circumvent my covenant

with his law

Dismiss my promise to my Lord

Tell me how to live the rest of my days

Sign here

Initial there

I hear the shackles from my wrist as I grab the

pen

And sign some Mickey Mouse signature to bring

this to an end

Because this can't be happening

This can't be real

With the last stroke of the pen

I hear my sentence

What my judge and juror feel is sufficient and
appropriate for me

Forget time already served for good behavior

Let's neglect the community service done

No

The sentence I share is the same as those who
commit the most disturbing crimes to society

LIFE.....with the possibility of parole.

Chapter 26 – Life

Losing your loved one is not easy; especially if you have no control over the situation. First you take it out on them. You begin to blame them for not doing this or doing that. Or maybe if they would have done more of this or that, it could have worked out. Next you begin self-reflection, examining the entire relationship and questioning everything you have done. Was I attentive enough? Did I show support of what brought them joy? Was I a good listener? There was that time I forgot what she had just said to me because I was looking at the ball game; I wonder if that could have been it. Or was I too needy? Did I smoother him by always making us do things together? Did I become boring? I did stop hanging with my friends to work on my relationship. What could it have been? Sooner or later, you feel as if you are confined to prison, but it is the prison of your mind and heart.

As hard as it is to cultivate a loving relationship, it is just as hard to lose one. You begin to look to ease the pain any way you can. Some begin to drink. Others may turn to sex as a way to remove the hurt and love for the other person. No matter what your vice becomes, you have to deal with the reality. You alone decide where your life will go. Yes, for a time, someone else can control certain situations and the outcomes in your life, but how will you deal with the outcome? How long will you let that decision eat at you? Soon it begins to possess you. When you are ready, you can remove yourself from your self-made prison and begin to enjoy life.

Chapter 27

I Am An Asshole

I Am An Asshole

I am an asshole
This term has been used to describe me in so
many ways
But those that define me as an asshole
Can they really say that I'm an asshole?
Am I an asshole by the confidence in myself?
Some call it cockiness
Others may call it conceit
I call it being me
For so long people degraded and belittled me
So why shouldn't I think highly of me?
Am I an asshole?
Am I an asshole because I put my lady first?
You see I tried and tried to give her everything
Things she wanted
Things I wanted for her
But the more I pushed and pushed the universe
pushed back
And said 'not yet'

But I still pushed and pushed

And I pushed her away

Am I an asshole because I want more?

Settling for anything except the best is

unacceptable

But so many are content with being average

They see my drive and determination

And I'm the asshole.

Am I an asshole because I live by a code?

A code we as men should have learned a long

time ago

Your girl is always your girl in my eye

And with all the different colors, shapes and

sizes,

Why do I need your girl?

So when brothers who were my friend, my pal,

my associate fucks with my girl

I can't fuck with you

I can't fuck with you because you showed me

ass is more important

So I say to you, fuck you,

But I'm the asshole.

Am I an asshole because I'm honest?

I speak the truth

So don't think you can change me

When I say I'm not looking for anything

Sex is not going to change my mind

What you have between your legs will never

have me succumb

You saw what you wanted to see

And believed what you wanted to believe

But at the end of the day

I always said you don't want to be with me

But I'm an asshole.

Am I an asshole because I'm guarded?

A defense I mastered a long time ago

To avoid the pitfalls of love and relationships

Many years ago one part of my heart was gone

The disease we call cancer took part of my

heart

And as a babe I can't even remember uttering

the words,

Daddy, dad or father

Vague memories of a man I never knew

Taken from me too soon

Am I an asshole?

Because he was taken from me

But through it all my best friend was there

Every day I was by her side

Holding on to every word she said as if it was

the gospel of Grandma

And no matter what was going on she was there

Ultimately all good things must come to an end

And my best friend and my heart was gone

Ten years old and I'm all alone

My father and grandmother

Both gone

So am I an asshole?

Because I had to grow up alone

Alone in the sense that no one knew me

Understood me

Guided me

So my best offense became a great defense

Never again would I allow myself to feel hurt or
pain
Over and over I had to endure loss at such a
young age
And with the elements of drugs, sex and violence
Circling me everyday
I withdrew deeper and deeper into a place no
man should see
But I did
I was there
But am I an asshole?
Because on one fateful day I decided to say I do
To a creature that fulfilled my every desire
And I shed that darkness for the light
Let down my guard and felt
All the feelings I suppressed for years and years
Relinquished to you and yours
But it was too much
I tried too hard
To be the husband, father and friend I never
had

But as easily as it came, it too was soon gone

Again

Alone

Am I really an asshole?

If being an asshole means I try to better myself

Protect myself

Provide for my family

Hold a code of integrity and honor

And be truthful and faithful

Well in your world I'm an asshole

But I'm not an asshole

I'm just misunderstood.

Chapter 27 - I Am an Asshole

One should never judge a book by its cover but, as humans, we cannot help ourselves. We see in a person what we want to see. Sometimes we completely ignore their cries for help. The smile we see is perhaps a mask for the tragedy they are going through. That laugh may be a cry for the pain on the inside. These are the masks we show so we are not judged. But what if we show how we really are? Will people accept us, or judge?

We all have our pasts -- our skeletons -- we try to forget. It's not as easy for some as it is for others. So these become the assholes. *You should just get over it and move on. It's your choice to hold on to the past, so you're unhappy because you want to be.* These statements are true, but there are also things called emotional scars. Many times we go through adulthood without understanding why we think or act the way we do. It's important to remember that our past made us who we are. If we don't understand the issues we have early in life, we develop bad habits. It's not the asshole's fault. They are just misunderstood.

Only God knows you. Only God understands you. Only God can judge you. These are not assholes. The real assholes are those who don't understand their own issues and prefer to label others.

The Conclusion

Conclusion

This journey of life has many twists and turns, ups and downs. In truth, we have to make the best of it because we only get to do it once -- there are no do-overs. We must take advantage of every situation and make the most out of it.

The goal of this book is to not just entertain you through poetry but, hopefully, help you open your eyes to what you have in front of you. We all have trying times, but they are only temporary. We must start to prepare our minds and hearts for when things get back on track. We do that through life lessons. It's similar to the glass half-empty or half-full perspective. If you look at your current situation as hopeless then you're already defeated. Instead, learn from the situation, decide how you would have done things differently, pray, reflect and move on. At this point, it's out of your control.

Each one of us has something to give back. My personal life lesson is to have experienced the hurt, pain, loss and heartache to help make your life better. It's my job to take my life experiences and observations, turn them into lessons, and share them with you. My lessons of life are no different from yours, except I put my life to poetry. Things I can't talk about with others -- things I have held inside for years -- need to be said and shared.

As a father of a daughter, I want her to understand how to behave as a woman, how she needs to portray herself as a lady, as well as ensure whomever she decides to be with appreciates her as a lady. For my son, I have to prepare him to be a man. Since I've lost the capability of being with him every day, I have to work twice as hard. I am his example of what and what not to do. I never want him to experience my mistakes, because he will already have to account for his own errors. Somehow I have to show him how to be a gentleman to women, and the proper way to carry himself as a strong, respectable man.

Again, life is a roller coaster. We have our ups and downs. How good the up times are is a reflection of how well we respond to our down times. One thing to remember on this ride is that you don't have to do it alone. Family, friends, wives and/or husbands are there for us to try to make this ride as enjoyable as possible. Yes, there will be some scary moments -- especially when we are on top of the mountain looking down at the valley ahead. But before you despair, look to the left, right, or behind, and you will see someone willing to share their voice and give you their life lesson.

About the Author

Trenell Harris is a rising poetic voice offering a fresh spin on life, love, and relationships. His freshman release, The Silent Voice: Life Lessons through Poetry, reveals a perspective that is down-to-earth, inspiring, humorous and, at times, heartbreaking.

Growing up on Chicago's South Side, Trenell began writing at an early age as means of coping with the harsh realities of inner-city life. The son of a single mother, he developed his wisdom and insight through years of keen observation and life experience as he journeyed from the gritty streets of his childhood to the privileged halls of corporate America.

Today, Trenell continues to be a passionate and prolific writer, with his first novel, Black Couch Confessions, scheduled for release in 2015. He is also a former model, entrepreneur, and scholar with multiple degrees, as well as numerous honors and awards. In his spare time, the devoted father of two enjoys playing sports and spending time with his children. He currently resides in Atlanta, Georgia with his family. To learn more about the life and work of Trenell Harris, visit www.the-silent-voice.com or www.facebook.com/the.silent.voice7.

27598150R00103

Made in the USA
Charleston, SC
17 March 2014